THE SECOND WORLD WAR IN THE AIR IN PHOTOGRAPHS

1941

L. ARCHARD

AMBERLEY

Acknowledgements

I would like to thank Campbell McCutcheon, John Christopher and Amberley Publishing, without whose image collections this book would not have been possible. In the main text, unless otherwise indicated, images are from the J&C McCutcheon Collection. In the colour section, unless otherwise indicated, images are courtesy of Amberley Publishing.

First published 2014

Amberley Publishing
The Hill, Stroud
Gloucestershire, GL5 4EP

www.amberley-books.com

British Library Cataloguing in Publication Data.
A catalogue record for this book is available from the British Library.

ISBN 978 1 4456 2241 5 (print)
ISBN 978 1 4456 2264 4 (ebook)

Typesetting and Origination by Amberley Publishing.
Printed in Great Britain.

Introduction

The year 1941, in many ways, was the one in which the Second World War truly became a world war, and at the end Britain had two new and significant allies in the fight against Nazi Germany, although there was a new enemy as well: imperial Japan.

The year had begun much as the previous one had ended – with the Luftwaffe's bombing campaign against British cities. However, it has been suggested that at the start of 1941, the combination of German losses and the effective use of countermeasures to block the German navigation aids meant that the Luftwaffe switched its focus to coastal targets, which were easier to find. This continued into the early summer, after which the short nights and the forthcoming offensives in the Balkans and, more significantly, the Soviet Union meant that German activity over Britain dropped as the Luftwaffe bomber squadrons were redeployed.

In the spring of 1941, RAF Fighter Command went on the offensive, launching fighter sweeps by 'big wings' of aircraft over northern France, which were known as Rhubarb missions. The idea was to bring the battle to the German fighter squadrons, only the Luftwaffe failed to oblige as expected. As a further temptation, bombers were added to the mix, but thanks to German flak, casualties were heavy.

The bombers were also flying on the strategic missions against Germany for which they had been designed. However, an analysis of target reports and photographs from 100 different raids between June and July 1941 revealed that only a third of the crews who had claimed to hit the target on their raid had got within 5 miles of the aiming point, and that moonlight was essential to help find the target. New four-engined heavy bombers, the Short Stirling and the Handley Page Halifax, were coming into service with the RAF, but the German defences were improving too; there was a chain of radar stations, flak batteries, searchlights and night fighters, known as the Kammhuber Line, that defended the Dutch and German coasts. Despite the casualties and the issues with accuracy, however, the bomber offensive was a major prop to morale in Britain, as the bomber crews seemed to be the only people who could hit back against the Germans, and critics of Bomber Command voiced objections at their peril.

In the war at sea, aircraft played a key role in the *Bismarck*'s lone sortie out into the Atlantic. It was a Catalina flying boat that first sighted the German battleship on 26 May 1941. Later, a Catalina would mount a twenty-seven-hour-long continuous surveillance.

In an attempt to slow down the *Bismarck*, two sorties were launched by Fleet Air Arm Swordfish torpedo bombers; the first, from HMS *Victorious*, had no noticeable effect, but the second, a few days later, mounted by aircraft from HMS *Ark Royal*, did score a success, damaging the *Bismarck*'s steering gear and slowing her enough for the pursuing warships of the Home Fleet to catch her and deal the *coup de grâce*.

The main role of aircraft in the Atlantic, however, was patrolling against U-boats. The mainstay of Coastal Command's long-range patrol aircraft had been the Short Sunderland flying boat, but American-made aircraft were now coming to the fore: the above-mentioned Consolidated Catalinas that followed the *Bismarck*, along with their stablemates the Consolidated B-24 Liberators and the Boeing B-17 Flying Fortresses. All three played an important role in narrowing the mid-Atlantic gap, the area that aircraft flying from either side of the ocean had previously been unable to reach. The gap was further narrowed by a reconnaissance squadron that moved to Iceland, taken under the control of Britain, and later of the US following the fall of Denmark to the German invasion in April 1940.

However, Coastal Command's were not the only aircraft patrolling the North Atlantic: the U-boats, too, had air cover. An experienced bomber group was put at the disposal of Admiral Dönitz, the U-boat commander, and Focke-Wulf Condor aircraft could now patrol from bases across the Atlantic seaboard of most of Europe. Although the Condors played a role in locating convoys that the U-boats could attack, and indeed carried bombs so that they could mount attacks on their own account, the air cover for the U-boats was not on the same scale as that for the convoys.

Further to the south, in the Mediterranean, there was also considerable aerial activity. Italian forces had invaded Greece in late October 1940, but quickly became bogged down, while the Italian forces in North Africa were being routed by a British force led by General O'Connor. Hitler realised that Germany was going to have to come to its ally's rescue, and so in March 1941 German forces invaded Yugoslavia, through which they would have to travel to reach the Italians in Greece. Yugoslav forces offered little resistance to the Germans, and they quickly reached Greece, overwhelming the British force that had been able to help the Greeks to resist the Italians. The RAF's Gladiators, Hurricanes and Blenheims proved inadequate in the face of the German onslaught.

After British forces were evacuated from mainland Greece in April 1941, the Germans turned their attention to the island of Crete, which had been used as a stepping stone for the British forces that had gone to Greece from North Africa. On 20 May 1941, the Germans used their airborne forces to launch a massive assault on Crete. Intelligence from messages encrypted by Enigma and then successfully decrypted revealed the intent to attack Crete, and so the defenders were prepared. The Germans suffered heavy casualties in the early days of the assault, and although they eventually triumphed, it was a pyrrhic victory to say the least. The Royal Navy escorted convoys bringing reinforcements and also covered the evacuation of the remaining Allied troops from Crete, suffering heavy casualties as a result.

The Germans were also intervening in North Africa. In March 1941, elements of what would become the Afrika Korps landed in Libya. As well as tanks, Rommel brought the Luftwaffe with him, and his Junkers Ju 87 Stukas were in action from the start of his offensive on 1 April. British forces were quickly pushed back; within three weeks, they would be driven back from El Agheila in western Libya to Egypt, from where they had started. Forces from the Eighth Army, however, still held the strategically important port of Tobruk, and the city would be besieged and under constant air attack until it was relieved in December 1941.

Yugoslavia and the Balkans and Rommel's campaign in North Africa would fade almost into insignificance in what would follow: on 22 June, at 3.15 a.m., the Luftwaffe bombed major cities in the area of Poland occupied by the Soviets. German troops followed, crossing the border and achieving complete surprise. After the war, the German generals would claim that the invasion of Yugoslavia had been an unnecessary delay to Barbarossa, and that given more days of summer in which to fight, their men could have won. This was all to come, however; as the invasion started, things were looking bleak for the Soviets. In terms of the air war, the Luftwaffe had been charged with neutralising the Soviet Air Force and achieving air superiority, and this they did spectacularly. The Soviets had concentrated their aircraft rather than dispersing them, and the Luftwaffe claimed to have destroyed almost 1,500 enemy aircraft on the first day alone; when the Germans checked the wreckage left behind on the airfields, this would prove to have been a conservative estimate. One of the many warnings that the Soviet High Command would receive, and ignore, about the Germans' intentions came from the hundreds of Luftwaffe reconnaissance flights that would cross the Soviet border before the invasion; Stalin forbade the Soviet Air Force from intercepting them.

As well as not being ready for war, their aircraft lined up neatly on their aerodromes, the Soviet Air Force had other problems. Many of its aircraft were obsolete, and the new models starting to come off the production lines were inferior to the German aircraft. There were human problems as well: the upper echelons of the Soviet armed forces had been decimated in the Purges between 1936 and 1938, executed or sent to the Gulags, and their replacements were young, inexperienced and understandably reluctant to take the initiative. There were problems lower down the chain of command, too – an order in December 1940 commanded that flight training be shortened and accelerated. An investigation into the high accident rate in the Soviet Air Force led to its commander, General Rychagov, being removed from his post shortly before the German invasion. He would be arrested shortly after the invasion, and was executed in late October. Hitler's comment was, 'We have only to kick in the door and the whole rotten structure will come crashing down.' Many analysts agreed with him.

The result of all this was that the Luftwaffe would have total air superiority over the Eastern Front for the rest of 1941 and could devote itself almost fully to providing close air support for the troops on the ground. Strong close air support helped the Germans to destroy attempted Soviet counter offensives, for instance at the Battle of Brody, which lasted four days from 26 June and was one of the largest tank battles in history, and at a Soviet attempt to counter attack during the Battle of Smolensk later in the summer. However, German air superiority did not mean that the Soviet Air Force, or indeed Soviet anti-aircraft gunners, stopped resisting and by the time of the German offensive against Moscow from October to December 1941 – Operation Typhoon – the Luftwaffe had suffered heavy losses. As the winter wore on, the weather conditions deteriorated to the point at which the Luftwaffe could not continue operating in support of the troops on the ground.

German losses might have been heavy, but Soviet losses of course were heavier still. The problem for the Germans was that before the war, as part of the Five Year Plans for Soviet industrialisation in the 1930s, a lot of new industrial facilities were constructed east of the Ural Mountains, in Siberia. After the war started, many further industrial facilities were moved wholesale from the western Soviet Union. The Luftwaffe did not have a long-range heavy bomber that could reach these targets; the so-called Uralbomber project, which could have yielded a German equivalent to the Avro Lancaster or the Boeing B-17 Flying Fortress, had been sacrificed to the Luftwaffe's internal politics and the belief that the German army would not have to fight a campaign that would require such an aircraft. So, the Soviet armed forces were able to replenish themselves from factories far beyond the reach of the Wehrmacht and launch a counter-offensive in the winter of 1941 that would drive the exhausted German armies back from Moscow.

In December 1941, just as the German offensive against Moscow was grinding to a halt, the war widened yet again. On Sunday 7 December 1941, 'a date which will live in infamy' as Roosevelt put it, aircraft of the Imperial Japanese Navy attacked the US Pacific Fleet in its base at Pearl Harbor on the Hawaiian island of Oahu. One of the planners of the attack, Captain Minoru Genda, had been the Japanese naval attaché in London at the time of the Royal Navy's attack on the Italian fleet in its anchorage at Taranto and studied the attack carefully. Simultaneously, Japanese forces attacked a range of targets across Asia and the Pacific, including Hong Kong and Shanghai, what was then Malaya, the Philippines and the islands of Wake and Guam. The Japanese had been under sanctions imposed on them by the United States in response to their undeclared war in China, and the Japanese had hoped to mount a swift campaign to seize colonial territories in Asia and the Pacific that could provide the resources they needed, including the oil-rich Dutch East Indies or Indonesia and the British colony of Malaya, rich in rubber. Britain and the US, among other countries, declared war on Japan on 8 December, the day after Pearl Harbor. On 11 December, Germany and Italy declared war on the United States, and the US government reciprocated. Meanwhile, in an effervescent spree of conquests through the last weeks of 1941, the Japanese invaded the British colonies of Burma, Malaya and Hong Kong, the islands of Borneo and Sumatra, the American protectorate of the Philippines and the US naval bases of Guam and Wake Island in the Pacific.

Japanese air power, particularly Japanese naval aviation, was the key to this success, overwhelming the often inadequate air defences of their targets and establishing air superiority. The importance of air superiority became clear on 10 December when Japanese bombers attacked and sank the Royal Navy battleship *Prince of Wales* and the battlecruiser *Repulse* off the coast of Malaya. Patrick Bishop has suggested that Churchill had intended *Prince of Wales* and *Repulse* to have had a similar deterrent effect on the Japanese as the German battleship *Tirpitz* had on Britain, but as would happen to *Tirpitz* herself later in the war, air power would prove dramatically superior.

January

In the early months of 1941, the RAF continued its attacks against the German forces in northern France and the Low Countries to disrupt potential invasion plans. This photograph shows bomb damage to buildings that had been used as barracks for German troops on the French coast.

Bremen, on the northern coast of Germany, was attacked by RAF bombers on the night of
1 January 1941. The target was the city's Focke-Wulf aircraft factory. This photograph shows
the city's docks prior to the attack.

An artist's impression of the air raid on Bremen.

As well as the war in northern Europe, the war continued in the Mediterranean as well. This photograph shows three Italian Savoia-Marchetti SM. 77 bombers flying over the town of Candia on Crete.

Bomb damage in the Greek town of Kastoria.

The aircraft carrier HMS *Ark Royal* conducting flying operations in the Mediterranean.

On 10 January 1941, a convoy carrying supplies to Greece, escorted by the aircraft carrier HMS *Illustrious*, was attacked by Luftwaffe dive-bombers based on the island of Sicily. Aircraft carriers were vital in diverting convoys, particularly in the Mediterranean, much of which was dominated by the Axis.

The Blitz against British cities continued. This image shows nurses examining the damage to a London hospital.

Free French sailors help to clear away the debris in Portsmouth following a heavy raid on 10 January.

Two images showing captured German aircrew under guard and on their way to a PoW camp after one of the night air raids against British cities.

Retrieving letters from a postbox that had been buried beneath rubble in London's Paternoster Square, near St Paul's Cathedral. Images such as this were vital for propaganda purposes, showing that life was continuing despite the bombing.

An artist's impression of an air raid against Catania, on Sicily, on the night of 12/13 January 1941. Catania was used as a base for German and Italian attacks on British shipping in the Mediterranean.

Left: The wreck of an Italian Caproni CR.42 biplane fighter between Bardia and Tobruk in Libya.

Below: An Italian S.79 bomber that landed on the edge of Sidi Barrani airfield after being attacked by RAF fighters. Three of the bomber's crew were dead when it came down.

Above: B24 bombers under construction at the Consolidated Aircraft plant in San Diego, California. The B24 would prove extremely useful as a long-range patrol aircraft for Coastal Command.

Right: The crew of an anti-aircraft gun aboard a destroyer on alert, waiting for enemy aircraft to come into view.

Left: The effects of close air support in the Western Desert. This photograph shows Italian soldiers throwing themselves on the ground as a bomb explodes.

Below: In Albania, the Italians began to use aircraft rather than shipping to transport reinforcements for the army fighting the Greeks because of pressure on the sea link to Italy.

A bomber of the South African Air Force being refuelled in East Africa. South African troops played a key role in the campaign to force the Italians out of Abyssinia (now Ethiopia), which Italy had invaded in 1935.

A rather grainy image showing firefighters trying to put out flames after a heavy raid by the Luftwaffe against Plymouth. A major base for the Royal Navy, Plymouth was heavily bombed.

February

Bomb craters outside Tobruk, where the RAF had attacked defensive gun positions around the port prior to the assault in which the Italians were pushed out.

Four Spitfire pilots stand in a roadside field, examining the wreckage of a Ju 87 Stuka dive-bomber, which they came across while on patrol and attacked.

A photograph of the Italian air base at Addis Ababa, in what is now Ethiopia, following a raid by the RAF. The hangars are on fire and burning fiercely.

The ruins of London's Haberdashers' Hall following an air raid. Rebuilt after the Great Fire of 1666, wartime propaganda said that the hall had been burnt in a second Great Fire.

A stretcher party removing an injured person from the ruins of a bombed building.

A striking photograph of a London church
after an air raid.

An air raid from the German point of view.
This German gunner is looking out at two
Heinkel He 111s.

Lockheed Hudson bombers made for the RAF are seen here lined up at an airfield in California, ready for delivery.

A British pilot climbing out of an American-made Grumman Martlet fighter, designed for use on aircraft carriers. At this point in the war, the Martlet, the British name for what was more commonly known as the F4F Wildcat, was land-based but later in the year they would start operating from HMS *Audacity*, the first British escort carrier.

Right: An American-made Curtiss P-40 Tomahawk fighter in British markings, being unloaded from its crate after delivery.

Below: A British pilot preparing to take a Brewster Buffalo fighter for a test flight. The Buffalo was another US-made aircraft provided to Britain under Lend-Lease but would prove inadequate in both British and US service.

Left: A German Focke-Wulf Fw 200 Condor long-range bomber and patrol aircraft, used to attack Allied convoys in the Atlantic.

Below: An Italian seaplane, destroyed in an RAF bombing raid on a base at Bomba in Libya.

A photograph taken during an air raid on the port of Valona, part of the supply route for Italian troops fighting in Greece. The RAF played a key role, along with the Royal Navy, in disrupting the lines of communication between Italy and Albania, and on to Greece. Marked on the photograph are a military facility (A), a concentration of vehicles (B), trenches (C) and a hospital (D).

March

The Italian pilot and engineer of a Caproni 133 bomber, captured by Indian troops in Eritrea and flown to the Sudan by an RAF pilot; the two Italian airmen were carried as crew.

An Italian destroyer, sunk in the harbour at Benghazi, on the coast of Libya, by the RAF, seen after the fall of the city to British troops.

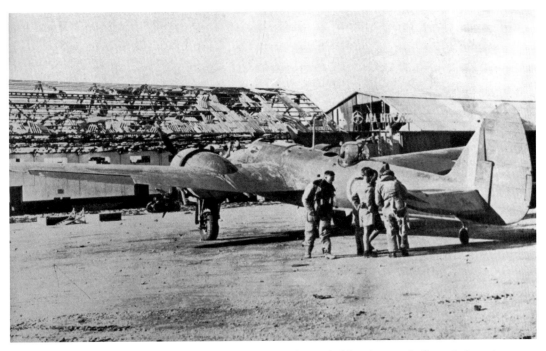

An RAF Blenheim bomber on the ground at Berka airfield, a former Italian air base just outside Benghazi.

Left: A Messerschmitt Bf 110 dropping two bombs on a ship, part of a convoy making its way up the east coast of Britain.

Below: The view from the convoy, with a bomb exploding in the sea behind one of the ships.

Above: A Czechoslovakian bomber crew walking past a load of bombs as they make their way to their aircraft. One of the largest groups of non-British personnel in the RAF came from Czechoslovakia.

Right: A wonderful photograph of a Wellington bomber from a Czechoslovakian bomber squadron in the RAF flying by moonlight.

Two gunners from a Wellington bomber help each other to put on their electrically heated clothing. On a mission of some five or six hours, at high altitude, especially in winter, this equipment would be essential to avoid frostbite, hypothermia or worse.

Douglas Boston bombers undergoing completion in the United States before delivery to Britain. In March 1941, Churchill made his famous speech asking the Americans for 'the tools to finish the job'. The Boston, known as the A-20 Havoc, was used as a light bomber, for attacking shipping and to support night fighter operations, carrying a powerful searchlight.

A group of RAF night fighter pilots before taking off on their next flight; three of them are seen wearing darkened goggles to accustom their eyes to the darkness.

Take-off on a night fighter airfield. A pilot is climbing into a Hurricane, lit by bright moonlight.

Searching for survivors amid the rubble of Clydeside following a raid on the night of 14/15 March 1941. The town of Clydebank, a centre for ship building and munitions production, was almost completely destroyed in what became known as the Clydebank Blitz. Only seven houses in the town reportedly remained undamaged.

Bomb damage in a town in the north-west of England. This woman is rescuing what belongings she can from the ruins of her home.

Right: A German drawing, published in *Die Woche,* showing a Dornier Do 17 over central London. In this view of the war, London's defences seem to have consisted mostly of searchlights.

Below: A German bomber, loaded with bombs, just taxiing to take off for a raid against Birmingham.

Above: German anti-aircraft guns firing at night.

Left: A photograph showing a raid by the RAF on Emden, on the north-west coast of Germany, very close to the Dutch border, on 31 March. This was the first of many Allied bombing raids on the city, the main sea port for the Ruhr.

April

The crew of a Sunderland flying boat that had made a forced landing off the coast of Iceland had to drain their petrol tank, remove it and clean it before the aircraft could take off and return to its base in Scotland. With a range of over 1,900 miles, Sunderlands often mounted long patrols over the North Atlantic.

Winston Churchill visiting bomb-damaged homes in Bristol.

A street in Birmingham following two successive nights of bombing.

The king and queen visiting the victims of a raid in the East End of London.

The wreck of a German Junkers Ju 88 bomber washed up on a beach following a night raid.

Left: A crewman checking a rack of flares carried on a Saro Lerwick flying boat on patrol over the North Atlantic.

Below: A US-built Consolidated Catalina flying boat. With a range of some 4,000 miles, the Catalina was vital for protecting the Atlantic convoys, at this time suffering heavily from the depredations of the German U-boats.

German airmen undergo a briefing after arriving at an airfield in North Africa. The squadron's
Bf 110s sit in the background.

Another image, not of great quality, showing a Bf 110 in the desert with camels in the foreground.

Luftwaffe men sit in deckchairs in the North African desert while supplies are unloaded from a transport plane in the background.

An airfield in Sicily used by the Luftwaffe. Bombs are laid out in rows in the foreground of this photograph while a bomber sits in the background.

Above: This photograph shows heavy bomb damage in Plymouth. Most of the city's children were evacuated in 1941 and thousands more of the population moved out to the fringes of Dartmoor when a raid was expected.

Right: The success of the German paratroopers in the Low Countries persuaded Churchill to form a British airborne force. This photograph shows a group of potential paratroopers around the hole through which they would practise making jumps while still on the ground.

Above: The next stage in the parachute training process. Paratroopers are seen making a jump from a flight of converted Armstrong Whitworth Whitley bombers.

Left: Paratroopers descending during a training excercise.

Two photographs showing an innovative means of protecting a convoy from the attentions of the Luftwaffe's dive-bombers. The upper image shows the convoy flying barrage balloons in an attempt to keep the Stukas from getting too close. The lower image shows a bomb exploding near to one of the ships.

May

On 10 May 1941 there was a full moon, and the RAF used the opportunity to mount what were described as heavy raids against targets in Hamburg, Berlin and elsewhere in Germany. This photograph shows a Wellington bomber taxiing up the runway, ready to take off.

Right: Rudolf Hess, who was deputy leader of the Nazi Party, and to whom Hitler had dictated the text of *Mein Kampf* while both men had been imprisoned in Landsberg Prison following the failure of the Beerhall Putsch in Munich in 1923.

Below: The wreckage of the Messerschmitt Bf 110 in which Hess flew to Scotland on 10 May 1941 in an attempt to open peace negotiations with Britain, something which Hitler regarded as one of the worst betrayals of his life.

German Junkers Ju 52 transports being prepared to carry paratroopers to the Greek island of Crete.

Paratroopers making their final preparations before embarking for Crete. The Battle of Crete would prove to be a pyrrhic victory for the German airborne forces, who suffered crippling casualties.

A German transport plane trailing smoke is about to crash near Heraklion, the largest city in Crete.

A crashed German glider on Crete with the bodies of two of the crew lying beside it.

Junkers Ju 52s crash-landed at Maleme airfield in the north-west of Crete in an attempt to get the paratroopers on the ground as quickly as possible.

Shipping in Suda Bay, on the northern coast of Crete, under attack by German dive-bombers during the early stages of the battle.

German gunners' views of the RAF in action. The image above shows a Spitfire going past a rear gun turret on a German bomber. The image below was taken from a gun turret on a Heinkel He 111.

Sink the *Bismarck*! Catalina flying boats of Coastal Command played a key role in helping to find *Bismarck* in the North Atlantic, while Swordfish torpedo bombers from the aircraft carrier *Ark Royal* hit the German battleship and damaged her steering gear enough to allow the pursuing Royal Navy ships to catch her.

Right: A photograph taken at a training
school for Home Guard officers shows
men practising firing at a low-flying
Westland Lysander. The effectiveness
of the Luftwaffe in the Blitzkrieg in
Poland, France and the Low Countries
had clearly not been forgotten as Britain
prepared for the possibility of invasion.

Below: The evacuation of Crete was
mostly carried out by ships, but aircraft
played a part as well. Here, a Sunderland
flying boat stands by to pick up a group
who have been rowed out from the
shore.

The Germans attacked the troops retreating from Greece, and especially from Crete. This spectacular photograph shows the barrage of anti-aircraft gunfire used to counter German air attacks in Greece.

Ludgate Hill in London, with St Paul's Cathedral in the background, following an air raid.

Firefighting boats on the River Thames giving a display during London's War Weapons Week. These boats were important for fighting fires in the centre of the city.

The church of St Clement Danes in the Strand, London, following repeated damage during air raids.

June

An RAF pilot climbing out of the cockpit of his Spitfire. In 1941, after the Battle of Britain, the RAF mounted offensive patrols over northern France, known as Rhubarb missions, but failed to bring the Luftwaffe to battle.

A series of photographs showing an attack by a Fleet Air Arm aircraft on German shipping off the Norwegian coast.

Above: A merchant ship viewed from a Sunderland flying boat of Coastal Command. Most merchant shipping travelled in convoy for protection but this ship appears to be alone, something that was permitted for ships which could travel too fast for the U-boats to catch.

Opposite: A photograph taken from an RAF Bristol Blenheim bomber as it attacks an Italian ship carrying what looks like a cargo of timber in the Mediterranean.

These two photographs show a Bristol Beaufort, known as *Wreck*, which claimed to have torpedoed a German pocket battleship off the coast of Norway on 13 June. The top image shows ground crew loading a torpedo on to the aircraft, while the bottom image shows the pilot posing beside the silhouette of the 'kill', newly painted on the side of the aircraft. Although the ship, *Lützow*, was not sunk, she did spend several months under repair following the attack.

A bomb from an RAF aircraft explodes near a fort at Rutba in Iraq, occupied by rebels who opposed British influence in the country, vital then as now for its oil supplies.

Night fighter pilots gathered around the stove in their ready room, waiting to be given orders to take off. The lights are dimmed to preserve the pilots' night vision and one seems to be wearing the dark goggles seen in the photograph on page 31.

Above: The ruins of London's Temple Church, built in 1185. The effigy shown in this photograph is that of Gilbert, the youngest son of William Mareschal, Earl of Pembroke.

Opposite: The church of St Mary-le-Bow, in London's Cheapside, burnt out after bombing raids.

Whitley bombers of the RAF being prepared for a bombing raid against Germany. The image above shows the aircraft being fuelled, and that below shows a 1,000-lb bomb being loaded into a Whitley's bomb bay. Although the Whitley was obsolete by the start of the war, it remained in service until suitable reinforcements arrived.

Preparing a Blenheim bomber for a sweep across the Channel into northern France. Blemheims were slow and vulnerable to German fighters and flak and many often took heavy casualties on daylight raids.

Bombs exploding on the runway of the airbase at St Omer-Longuenesse in northern France. Raids such as this were designed to tempt German fighters up to be destroyed by the bombers' escorts but this seldom worked and the bombers suffered from flak.

Above: Twin-engine bombers of the Soviet Air Force. At the start of Operation Barbarossa, the Luftwaffe outclassed their Soviet opponents and inflicted heavy losses.

Left: Lieutenant-General Pavel Rychagov, commander of the Soviet Air Force. He was removed from his post shortly before the German invasion as a result of an investigation into the high accident rate in the air force. He would be arrested shortly after the invasion and executed in late October 1941.

According to the caption on the front cover of this issue of *Signal*, the German propaganda magazine, the crew of this Junkers Ju 88 bomber had sunk seven ships in the Atlantic. (J&C McCutcheon Collection)

Opposite above: The Focke-Wulf Fw 200 Condor was a four engine monoplane originally designed as a long-range airliner; in 1938 a Condor made the first non-stop flight by a heavier-than-air aircraft between Berlin and New York. During the war, it was used for long-range maritime reconnaissance missions.

Opposite below: The Condors specialised in long missions over the North Atlantic, spotting and shadowing Allied convoys and reporting their position and course so that U-boats could move into position to attack them. Initially, Condors carried bombs to mount attacks of their own on the convoys, but losses meant that this was stopped.

Top: The fall of Norway and France meant that the Luftwaffe had access to bases on the Atlantic coast, increasing the range and duration of their patrols.

Der **Adler**

HEFT 9 · BERLIN, 29. APRIL 1941

PREIS **20 Pf.**
frei Haus 22 Pfennig

HERAUSGEGEBEN UNTER
MITWIRKUNG DES REICHS-
LUFTFAHRTMINISTERIUMS

**Vernichtungsschläge
im Südosten**

Großer Balkan-Bildbericht in diesem Heft

This issue of the Luftwaffe propaganda magazine *Der Adler* ('The Eagle') from April 1941, with its dramatic cover picture, promises an illustrated report on Stuka attacks in the Balkans, particularly on 'Fortress Belgrade'. (John Christopher Collection)

Opposite page: In May 1941, German airborne troops, the Fallschirmjäger, launched an assault on the Greek island of Crete. However, thanks to the code-breakers at Bletchley Park, Allied commanders were forewarned of the attack.

The coastline of Crete, as seen over the wing of a Junkers Ju 52 transport aircraft. The Germans suffered heavy casualties in the first wave of attacks on Crete, many of the Ju 52s being shot down and many paratroopers being shot and killed before they landed.

Fallschirmjäger resting on Crete. Once they landed, the German airborne troops faced resistance not only from the Allied troops defending the island but from the civilian population as well. Although the Germans eventually triumphed, it was a pyrrhic victory.

The distinctive shape of a Junkers
Ju 52 on an airfield in Sicily. Although the
Fallschirmjäger would see action throughout
the rest of the war, Crete would be the last
large-scale airborne operation mounted by the
Germans.

Another Junkers product. Ju 87 Stuka
divebombers on an airfield in Greece.
Overwhelming air superiority was, as usual, a
key factor in the successful German advance
south through Yugoslavia and Greece.

Aircraft carrier Italy

Italy requires no aircraft carriers. The whole of the Apennine Peninsula is the natural taking-off ground for a strong air force such as Italy has developed. Numerous bases on the islands in the eastern and western Mediterranean make it possible to carry out air attacks even on the enemy's most distant positions. The straits between Sicily and Tunis, Crete and Cyrenaica (in the middle of our picture) and also the waters round Gibraltar (front) which are more than 930 miles from Rome, and the vicinity of the Suez Canal (right, in the background) are daily and nightly the scene of conflicts in which the Italian Air Force, thanks to the central position of its base, plays a decisive part

PK. drawing:
Front Correspondent Hans Liska

'Aircraft carrier Italy'. This German propaganda image shows the Italians using their position in the middle of the Mediterranean to control the whole sea, from Gibraltar in the west to the Suez Canal in the east. (John Christopher Collection)

A very evocative image of a Dornier Do 17 flying over the Mediterranean. Although the location has not been given, the mountains mean that it could either be Italy or Greece.

The Germans would also cross the Mediterranean to help their Italian allies. The atmospheric image above shows a Messerschmitt Bf 110 circling above the palm trees at an airfield somewhere in North Africa. The image below shows a Bf 110 in its desert camouflage.

Above: A wonderful photograph of four Messerschmitt Bf 109 fighters racing over the sand as they take off. The Afrika Korps, including Luftwaffe forces, would change the situation in North Africa dramatically, forcing British troops back through the territory they had taken from the Italians.

Left: Luftwaffe pilots, some wearing sun helmets, gather round the nose of a Bf 110 as they enjoy a smoke and a chat somewhere in North Africa.

Luftwaffe mechanics work on a Bf 110, using a winch to lift heavy parts, while Junkers Ju 87 Stukas sit in the background, surrounded by fuel drums. Fuel supply would soon become a problem for the German forces in North Africa.

Left: On 22 July 1941, the Germans launched their biggest Blitzkrieg operation to date, the invasion of the Soviet Union. This photograph shows an aircraft circling over a German tank column as it advances through the USSR. (J&C McCutcheon Collection)

Below: The Germans encircled huge numbers of Soviet soldiers as they advanced, using air power to destroy counter-attacks. This view from the window of a Fiesler Storch communications aircraft, especially valuable in the USSR given the distances and bad roads, shows long lines of prisoners moving westwards. (John Christopher Collection)

Above: German ground crew prepare a Heinkel He 111 for a mission over the USSR. Although the Luftwaffe, as ever, played a key role in the Blitzkrieg, their bombers did not have the range to reach the Soviet industrial facilities east of the Urals, so the flow of men and material to the Red Army was secure.

Below: Despite this, the Luftwaffe could and did destroy vast quantities of Soviet equipment. Hans-Ulrich Rudel, a Stuka divebomber pilot, sank the Soviet battleship *Marat* in Kronstadt harbour, near Leningrad, in September 1941. (John Christopher Collection)

The pilot of this Messerschmitt Bf 109 is updating his tally on the tail of his machine. Thanks to the superiority of Luftwaffe pilots and aircraft at the start of Barbarossa, over 100 German fighter pilots claimed three-figure numbers of victories during the Second World War.

Photographs of aircrew from the Soviet
Baltic Fleet air arm. The Baltic fleet
would play a key role in the defence of
Leningrad.

July

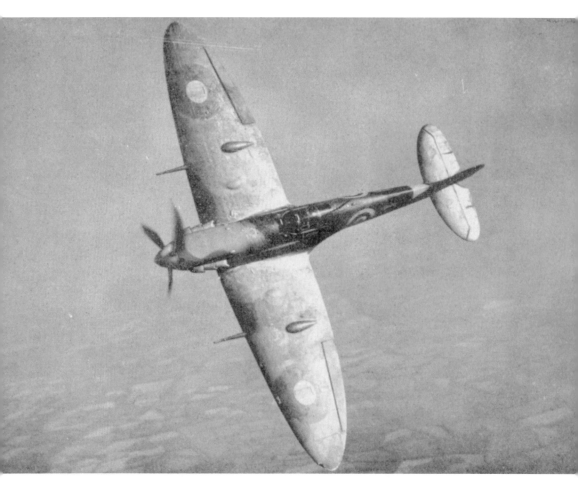

A view of one of the new models of Spitfire that started to come into service in 1941. In an improvement on the earlier Spitfires, the new Mark VB aircraft were armed with cannon.

A photograph showing the result of a daylight sweep by the RAF over northern France. The target was a power station.

A four-engined Focke-Wulf Condor, attacked and shot down by a Coastal Command aircraft just prior to launching an attack on a convoy.

Left: Russian ground crew load bombs onto an aircraft in preparation for a sortie against the invading Germans. German air superiority would make operations like this costly at the start of Barbarossa.

Below: A German column inside the Soviet Union following an attack by Soviet bombers.

Three images showing a low-level raid against Rotterdam docks. The first shows the aircraft – Bristol Blenheims – flying low over the Netherlands; the second shows the harbour of Waalhaven from over the tailplane of one of the aircraft; the third seems to show Dutch civilians cheering as the aircraft pass overhead.

Two photographs of an RAF bomb store. For some time, the bombing campaign against Germany and occupied Europe was the main way in which Britain could hit against its enemy.

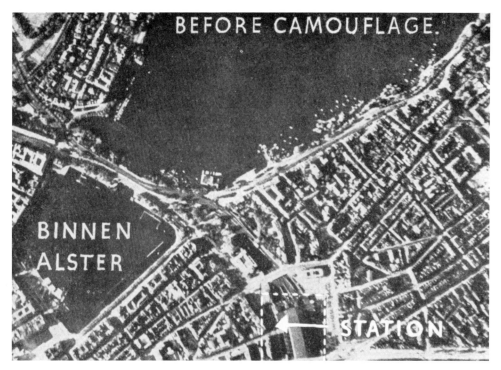

Two interesting photographs giving an example of camouflage as a defence against bombers. These two images show the Binnenalster, one of the two artificial lakes in the German city of Hamburg, covered with floating rafts intended to simulate a built-up area.

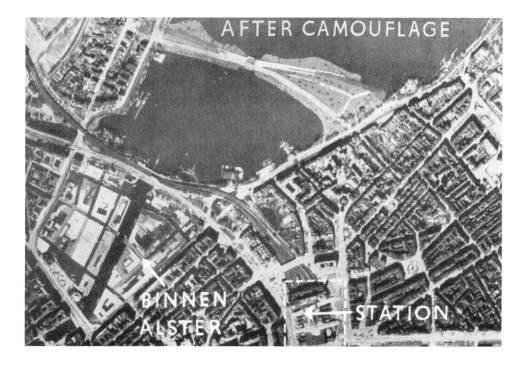

Above: Stalin watches as the Soviet Foreign Minister, Molotov, signs a pact of mutual assistance with Britain. The British ambassador, Sir Stafford Cripps, is standing beside Stalin.

Left: A plume of smoke rising from a bombed town somewhere in the Soviet Union.

Right: Captain A. Vyaznikov, an ace fighter pilot of the Soviet Air Force. The Germans, despite their superiority, did not have things all their own way and the Luftwaffe had suffered heavy casualties in the east by the end of the year.

Below: The wreckage of a crashed German bomber surrounded by curious villagers somewhere in the Soviet Union.

Two images showing aircrew on board a B24 Liberator bomber being flown across the Atlantic to Britain. The first Liberators served with Coastal Command, their long range of over 2,000 miles making them invaluable in the war against the U-boats.

The wreckage of a Messerschmitt Bf 109F being recovered from field somewhere in Britain.

August

The first Canadian bomber squadron, made up of airmen trained under the Empire Training Scheme, was formed in Britain in 1941. This photograph shows members of the squadron getting out of a lorry and climbing into their Wellington bomber.

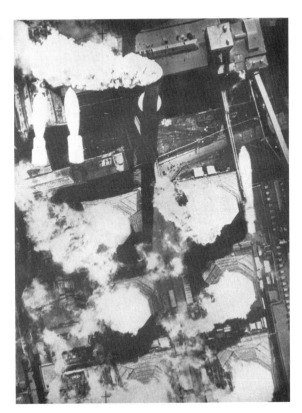

A daylight, low-level raid by the RAF on
12 August against two power stations near
Cologne. Of the fifty-four Blenheims that
took part, twelve were lost, 22 per cent.
The sustainable loss rate was 5 per cent.

Two female pilots transferring a plane from the factory to an RAF station. Female pilots were becoming increasingly common in these roles.

A tanker attacked in a Nowegian fjord by a Bristol Beaufort of Coastal Command. The ship was hit on the foredeck by a bomb and beached by her crew.

Above: A Soviet flying ambulance, transporting wounded soldiers back for medical treatment.

Right: A group of Soviet paratroopers who have just been dropped behind the German lines to attack the Germans from the rear, disrupting their lines of communication and supply. For the Germans, preventing attacks like this, both by regular Soviet troops and by partisans, would become an increasing problem.

Above: An aerial photograph of the city of Minsk, now in Belarus, devastated by artillery and air attacks.

Left: An armoured train moving up to the front line in the Soviet Union, with a soldier keeping watch for German aircraft.

Photographs showing a daylight attack by Short Stirlings on a target in France. The Stirling was the first British four-engined bomber to come into service during the Second World War. The upper image shows the bombers forming up with their escort of Hurricane fighters, while the bottom image shows bombs exploding on the target.

An interesting photograph showing battle-damaged Wellington bombers being repaired for further use. The Wellington's geodetic construction (clearly seen here) made it easy to repair, a key consideration in wartime.

The Dutch port of Rotterdam from a camera mounted on the belly of a Bristol Blenheim flying as low as 20 feet over the city in a raid on 28 August. Smoke can be seen rising from bombed ships in the middle distance.

Italian and German air power in the Mediterranean made it very difficult for Britain to maintain its lines of communications with bases in the region, particularly Malta. These two photographs show a young midshipman on a cruiser escorting a Mediterranean convoy watching for enemy aircraft, and an anti-aircraft gun crew at action stations.

Australian troops sheltering in a cave at Tobruk from the ever-present risk of enemy air attack. Tobruk was under seige for 240 days between April and November 1941, and subject to near constant shelling and bombing.

Above: A member of a Chinese military mission to the British colony of Malaya examines a Brewster Buffalo fighter. The Buffalo, acquired from the US, was thought to be sufficient to cope with Japanese aircraft; it would not be. China had been fighting an undeclared war with Japan since the Marco Polo Bridge Incident in July 1937.

Right: Looking down the barrel of an anti-aircraft gun at Tobruk.

September

Soviet troops picking through the wreckage of a German bomber brought down in a forest.

An aerial photograph showing an attack by Soviet aircraft against German artillery positions. Bombs can be seen falling to the left of the photograph, as can another of the Soviet aircraft.

The Messerschmitt Bf 109F of a German squadron commander, identified as Reinhardt Hein, after it was brought down by Soviet anti-aircraft fire.

Soviet anti-aircraft guns outside the Black Sea port of Odessa. The city was under siege by German and Romanian forces from August to October 1941.

The Soviet Baltic Fleet preparing to defend Leningrad (now St Petersburg) against a dive-bomber attack. The Baltic Fleet was an important part of the city's defences.

An anti-aircraft gun crew aboard the cruiser HMS *Suffolk* in the Arctic. The Arctic convoys to the Soviet Union were incredibly hazardous, in easy range of German air bases in northern Norway, travelling in twenty-four-hour daylight in the summer and through appalling weather conditions in the winter.

Part of the garrison of Tobruk manning a Bren gun concealed in a ruined house, waiting for the right moment to fire at German dive-bombers.

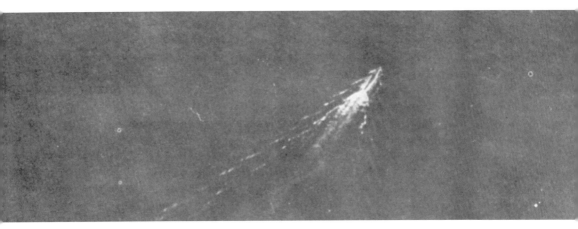

These two photographs show a U-boat spotted from the air by a Bristol Beaufort of RAF Coastal Command (*above*) and the disturbance in the water that suggested that the submarine had been hit by depth charges dropped by the Beaufort.

An aerial photograph showing an air raid on an industrial facility at Grand Quevilly, near Rouen, on 20 September. Bombs can be seen exploding on shipping in the river and on railway sidings, a chemical facility and a power station.

A Handley Page Halifax flies high above the clouds in this photograph. The Halifax was the second of the RAF's heavy bombers to come into service.

A rather unclear photograph showing a heavy attack by German and Italian aircraft on the aircraft carrier *Ark Royal* in the Mediterranean. In November, *Ark Royal* would be sunk by a U-boat in the Mediterranean while returnng from transporting aircraft to Malta.

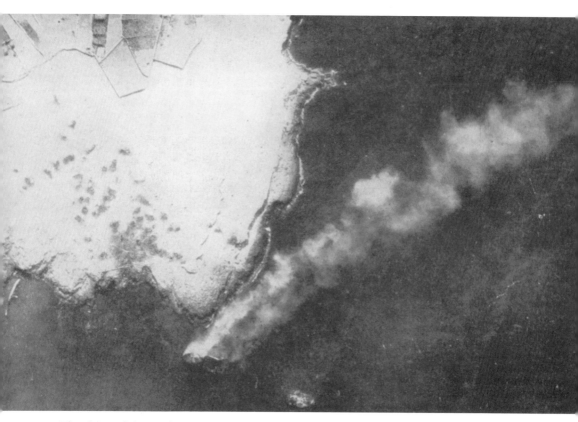

The shore of the Mediterranean island of Lampedusa. This photograph shows a 9,000-ton freighter that was attacked by Swordfish of the Fleet Air Arm and then set on fire in another attack, while a schooner that attempted to salvage the cargo is seen on its side to the left.

Two photographs showing the training of Polish paratroopers in the UK. Polish airborne troops would later serve with distinction on the Western Front.

The Hawker Hurricane Mk IIA, armed with four 20-mm Hispano cannon, came into service in 1941. These photographs show the aircraft in flight and a close-up of the armament.

A flying boat of the Soviet navy is being prepared by the ground crew for its next mission.

October

An air raid on the key Belgian port of Ostend on 3 October.

The defenders of Malta. The image above shows three sergeant pilots stationed on Malta, while the image below shows one of the Hurricane fighters flown by the island's defenders.

The striking photograph above shows a warship in the Mediterranean firing anti-aircraft guns on both sides as it defends itself from air attack, while the photograph below shows the wreckage of an Italian torpedo bomber shot down by aircraft from the carrier *Ark Royal* defending a convoy to Malta.

Aircraft carrier HMS *Illustrious* under attack from dive-bombers in the Mediterranean. The ship had to travel to the US to undergo repairs.

A Junkers Ju 87 Stuka dive-bomber in Italian markings, captured when it made a forced landing after running short of fuel.

Above: This photograph gives a good idea of the scale of the four-engined bombers coming into service with the RAF. This is a Short Stirling.

Left: Ground crew loading bombs into the bomb bay of a Stirling. The subdivisions in the bomb bay, which can be seen here, meant that the Stirling could not carry the 4,000 lb bombs used by the Lancasters and were one of the factors leading to the aircraft's withdrawal from the bomber offensive against Germany.

Right: A view inside the other RAF heavy bomber in service in 1941, the Handley Page Halifax. The figure in the bottom right is the radio operator, above him is the pilot and to the left of the pilot is the co-pilot. The Halifax had a crew of seven.

Below: A Halifax being prepared for a mission, with bombs being hoisted into the bomb bay. The Halifax, like the Stirling, had a sub-divided bomb bay that could not carry 4,000 lb bombs.

Above: A unit of Ilyushin Il-2 Shturmovik ground attack aircraft prepares to take off. The Shturmovik would become one of the most famous Soviet aircraft of the Second World War.

Left: A parade of young Soviet pilots.

A submarine in the Soviet naval base at Sevastopol on the Crimean Peninsula, which was heavily bombed and attacked by German artillery.

A Hawker Hurricane on an airfield in the Soviet Union. An RAF fighter wing was deployed to operate in the USSR to help the Soviet forces.

Some of the RAF pilots serving in the Soviet Union gathered around a wood fire. They seem to be waiting for water in a billy can suspended over the flames to boil.

A heavy air raid on Tobruk seen from a trench on the other side of the inlet on the Libyan coast on which the city stands.

The crew of a shot-down bomber is rescued from the Atlantic by a Short Sunderland flying boat. Thankfully the sea was calm enough to allow the flying boat to land.

November

A view over the wing of a Junkers Ju 57 Stuka dive-bomber, showing Perekop, the peninsula joining Crimea to the Soviet mainland. The pilot had been on a mission to provide close support to the German forces attacking the Crimea.

Two images showing a Heinkel He 115 seaplane being loaded with a torpedo, above, and, below, dropping its torpedo in an attack on a merchant ship in the Atlantic. Heinkel He 115s were mostly used to attack convoys to the Soviet Arctic ports but Soviet fighters and the introduction of escort carriers meant losses climbed.

Left: The Avro Manchester. Powered by two Rolls-Royce Vulture engines, which proved to be chronically unreliable, the Manchester was not a success. However, having been redesigned to carry four Merlins instead, it became the supremely successful Lancaster.

Below: The aircraft carrier HMS *Ark Royal* listing heavily after being torpedoed in the Mediterranean by a U-boat on 13 November.

Two views of Fairey Fulmar fighters on the aircraft carrier HMS *Victorious*. A descendant of the infamous Fairey Battle light bomber, the Fulmar suffered from being unwieldy although it could win victories against German and Italian fighters.

Above: An Atlantic convoy as seen from a US Navy flying boat escorting it away from the US coast.

Opposite: Inside an aircraft of the US Navy's Atlantic Patrol. The US Navy was starting to step up patrols off its east coast.

Left: The port of Nikolaiev, on the Black Sea coast of what is now Ukraine, following a German bombing raid.

Below: The devastating results of an attack by dive-bombers on a transport column on the Eastern Front.

Three Hawker Hurricanes of the RAF wing fighting in the Soviet Union.

The commander of a Soviet bomber gives instructions to his navigator and machine-gunner before taking off to mount an attack against the invading Germans.

Two images showing bomb damage on Malta, which by November 1941 had withstood somewhere in the region of 1,000 air raids.

RAF aircraft attack a German transport column in the Libyan desert in this artist's impression.

The battleship HMS *Nelson* in the Mediterranean, under attack by Italian torpedo bombers. One of the torpedo bombers can be see flying in the middle of the photograph to the right, and the splash close to the right edge of the photo marks where a torpedo has been dropped.

December

Admiral Nagano, chief of the Imperial Japanese Naval General Staff, was opposed to the Pearl Harbor attack but reluctantly gave his approval.

Above: A Japanese pilot's view of the Pearl Harbor attack, published in Germany's *Signal* magazine, showing fountains of water spurting into the air as the first bombs hit. (John Christopher Collection)

Opposite, top: Smoke rising from Hickam airfield, the USAAF base on the island of Oahu, attacked by the Japanese to prevent interference in the Pearl Harbor attack. Hickam was strafed by Mitsubishi A6M Zero fighters in the first wave, and then bombed and strafed again in the second wave.

Opposite, bottom: Smoke rising from the battleship USS *Arizona*, sunk during the Pearl Harbor attack with great loss of life. The *Arizona* was hit by four armour piercing bombs, one of which caused an explosion in the battleship's forward magazine.

A Japanese photograph showing Oklahoma class battleships under attack at Pearl Harbor. Seven of these ships were moored in what was known as Battleship Row, off Ford Island, including the ill-fated USS *Arizona*, top left. (John Christopher Collection)

Three targets attacked by the Japanese, on the same day as or very soon after the Pearl Harbor attacks. The top image shows the US naval base on the island of Guam, the middle image Kowloon, part of the British colony of Hong Kong and the bottom image Wake Island.

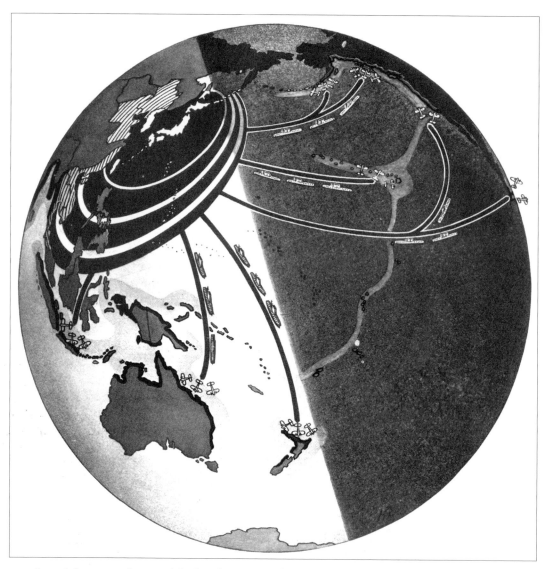

Japan's long arm. A map of the Pacific Ocean published in the German propaganda magazine *Signal* showing the theoretical reach of the Japanese navy's aircraft carriers, from Australia and New Zealand to the west coast of the United States and even what looks like Central America. (John Christopher Collection)

A 'Hurribomber' – a Hurricane fighter adapted to carry two 250-lb bombs and used successfully in North Africa. The Hurricane proved to be very adaptable to new armaments.

RAF bombers attacking a factory at Locri in Calabria, in the very south of Italy.

Hudson bombers flying over Iceland. Being able to use bases on Iceland, far out in the North Atlantic, meant that the area of the ocean that could be patrolled from the air was greatly increased.

Two very grainy images showing a merchant ship carrying supplies for the German and Italian forces in North Africa being bombed and sunk at sea by an RAF bomber. Maintaining a reliable supply line was a major problem for Rommel, commander of the Afrika Korps.

An unusual photograph showing RAF ground grew practising refuelling a Spitfire while wearing clothes to protect them from gas attack, still a matter of considerable concern to the British authorities.

A photograph showing an RAF raid against the German pocket battleships *Scharnhorst* and *Gneisenau* in Brest harbour on 18 December. These two warships were considered by the Admiralty to be a serious threat to the Atlantic convoys.